SACRAMENTO PUBLIC LIBRARY

Foundation

THIS BOOK WAS DONATED BY

The Sacramento Public Library Foundation
Books and Materials Endowment

The Sacramento Public Library gratefully acknowledges this
contribution to support and improve Library services in the community.

sac
IDb SACRAMENTO PUBLIC LIBRARY

EARTH'S INNOVATORS

INNOVATORS DEALING WITH NATURAL DISASTERS

Robyn Hardyman

LUCENT
PRESS

Published in 2020 by
Lucent Press, an Imprint of Greenhaven Publishing, LLC
353 3rd Avenue
Suite 255
New York, NY 10010

Produced for Lucent by Calcium
Designers: Paul Myerscough and Simon Borrough
Picture researcher: Rachel Blount
Editors: Sarah Eason and Jennifer Sanderson

Picture credits: Cover: Shutterstock: Konstantin Tronin; Inside: © Better Shelter: Jonas Nyström: p. 16; Märta Terne: p. 17; BuffaloGrid: p. 41; Tina Hovsepian/Cardborigami: pp. 1r, 22, 23; Courtesy of Concrete Canvas®: p. 19; DayOne Response, Inc.: pp. 30, 31; Flowminder Foundation, www.flowminder.org: p. 15; Gradian Health Systems: pp. 1cl, 35; Usama Kadri: p. 11; Life-bed: p. 28; LuminAID: pp. 42, 43; One Concern: p. 45; OX Global Vehicle Trust: p. 27; Peepoople.com: p. 24; Shutterstock: Arindambanerjee: p. 14; Frans Delian: pp. 1l, 10; Deepspace: p. 12; Fabiodevilla: p. 34; Julian Frees: pp. 1cr, 18; Alexander Ishchenko: p. 13; Nina Janesikova: p. 7; Victor Josan: p. 21; Udomporn Kaewsanguan: p. 20; Neenawat Khenyothaa: p. 8; KPG_Payless: p. 44; JEAN-FRANCOIS Manuel: p. 4; Masuti: p. 26; P11irom: p. 36; Alessandro Pietri: pp. 3, 38; Joseph Sohm: p. 6; Tong_stocker: p. 9; Chris Warham: p. 29; Dennis Wegewijs: p. 37; Worldpics: p. 33; SunFarmer: p. 39; Courtesy of TrapBag.com: p. 5; Jin Xie/Stanford University: p. 25.

Cataloging-in-Publication Data

Names: Hardyman, Robyn.
Title: Innovators dealing with natural disasters / Robyn Hardyman.
Description: New York : Lucent Press, 2020. | Series: Earth's innovators | Includes glossary and index.
Identifiers: ISBN 9781534565487 (pbk.) | ISBN 9781534565494 (library bound) | ISBN 9781534565500 (ebook)
Subjects: LCSH: Natural disasters--Juvenile literature. | Natural disasters--Safety measures--Juvenile literature. | Natural disasters--Prevention--Juvenile literature. | Natural disaster warning systems--Juvenile literature.
Classification: LCC GB5019.H37 2020 | DDC 363.34--dc23

Printed in the United States of America

CPSIA compliance information: Batch #BS19KL:
For further information, contact Greenhaven Publishing, LLC, New York, New York, at 1-844-317-7404.

Please visit our website, www.greenhavenpublishing.com.
For a free color catalog of all our high-quality books, call toll free 1-844-317-7404 or fax 1-844-317-7405.

Contents

CHAPTER 1

A TURBULENT WORLD

Living on our planet exposes us to dramatic natural events that can bring disaster. Earthquakes shake Earth at the places where its huge, moving pieces, called plates, meet each other. Volcanoes spew hot, molten lava over the land. Floods destroy homes and spread disease. Hurricanes and tornadoes tear across the land, leaving trails of destruction, and tsunamis bring great walls of seawater crashing onto the land.

Natural disasters bring chaos and tragedy to communities in all areas of the world, both rich and poor.

In a Year

In just one year, 2017, the world saw an earthquake in Mexico; flooding in India, Nepal, and Bangladesh; mudslides in Colombia, Hurricane Maria in the Dominican Republic and Puerto Rico; Hurricane Irma in the United States and the Caribbean; and Hurricane Harvey in Texas. Usually there is little we can do to stop these natural disasters from happening. They are forces of nature. Some disasters, such as extreme weather events, may become more frequent as our climate changes. Others, such as earthquakes and volcanoes, just happen.

Protection from Nature

There is a lot we can do to protect ourselves from natural disasters and to deal with the devastation they cause. Around the world people are using their science, technology, engineering, and math (STEM) skills and their creativity to find new ways to tackle the impact of natural disasters.

Solutions to these problems fall into three main categories. The first is prediction, which is knowing when a disaster looks likely to happen and warning people in the area. The second is safety, which is keeping people safe during an event, especially if it has been predicted. The third is relief. This is rescuing and caring for all the people the disaster affects. Relief is one of the biggest areas of innovation, as the problems these events cause can be so serious.

Building Defenses

There are some things that can be done to limit the damage a disaster such as an earthquake or a flood causes. Buildings can de designed to withstand the movement of minor earthquakes. Flood defenses can be put in place to protect built-up areas. U.S. innovator Everett Waid created a new flood-defense system after he saw the devastation caused by Hurricane Charley in 2004. His TrapBag is a series of large, pentagon-shaped bags, sloped on one side and vertical on the other. They are stacked side by side, and filled with a material that absorbs water. They use 40 percent less material than sandbags, and one section of TrapBag, which is 4 feet (1.2 m) high and 100 feet (30 m) long, replaces about 8,000 traditional sandbags. TrapBag is now widely used to protect against floods and mudslides.

TrapBags provide an effective defense against flooding along this shore.

Early Warning Systems

One of the most important things we can do to minimize the impact of natural disasters is to give people warning that one is about to happen. Early warning can prevent a natural disaster from turning into a major tragedy, with the loss of people's lives, homes, and belongings.

Detection

A fault line is where the plates of Earth's crust meet. When the plates rub against each other, it causes movement through the ground in a ripple effect. This ripple effect is an earthquake. Earthquake early warning systems have been in place in Mexico and Japan for years. They work by detecting the smallest movements deep underground at fault lines. Scientists developing early warning systems for earthquakes have found that the systems are more reliable at predicting small quakes than large ones.

Shake Alert

A new earthquake-detection system called ShakeAlert is being developed for the west coast of North America. ShakeAlert uses a combination of detectors in the ground and observations from satellites in space to provide the longest possible warning time for local people. For San Francisco, California, this may be about 50 seconds for a minor earthquake, or as little as 8 seconds for a major one. If the system is to be as sensitive as possible, there will be false alerts, but this is a price worth paying for longer notice of a real event.

Early warning of an earthquake can give people time to leave their homes.

When Mount Agung in Indonesia erupted in 2017, an early warning app helped people get to safety.

Another innovation in detecting earthquakes involves developing computers that use machine learning to predict them. Massive amounts of data from past earthquakes are fed into a complex system, so that it "learns" the conditions that occur shortly before an earthquake, and can recognize when another one is about to happen.

Volcano!

In Indonesia, Mount Agung is a huge volcano with a dangerous past. When it erupted in 1963, 1,100 people were killed. In November 2017, it started emitting huge gray and white clouds of ash, and the amount of magma, or hot molten rock, below the surface was growing.

In the past, loud sirens warned local people, but these could not be heard by everyone. The government's innovative early warning system now uses a network of cell phones. An app that people can download to their phones receives a signal, which makes the phone sound a loud siren alert when the volcano is likely to erupt. During the eruption in 2017, more than 100,000 people received the alert and fled the danger zone to safety.

Flood Alert

In some areas of the world, flooding is a constant challenge. The climate there brings heavy rain for weeks on end, known as the monsoon rains. Local people know when these rains are coming, but in some years, they are much more severe and their impact is much more serious. Early warning systems for such floods are being improved all the time.

Flood!

In Cambodia in Southeast Asia, the rainy season brings flooding every year. In 2013, however, the floods were much worse than usual. Floodwater covered almost half of Cambodia and affected nearly 1.7 million people. More than 50 people lost their lives and hundreds of thousands more were left homeless. An organization called People in Need has developed an early warning system that delivers warning messages directly to the cell phones of the people at risk. In the event of a natural disaster, Cambodia's National Committee for Disaster Management has been organized to send out warning messages to people in the affected areas. The system uses voice messages rather than text messages, which means that even if people cannot read, they are still warned.

These early warnings allow people to prepare themselves, their families, and their livelihoods for the oncoming danger. This could mean evacuation to the nearest safe site, or staying in their homes and securing their most important possessions—the extra time to prepare can often mean the difference between life and death.

In many countries in Southeast Asia, flooding is a regular occurrence during the rainy season.

INGENIOUS INNOVATIONS

Cambodia's flood-warning system would not be possible without the ingenious innovation of David Wilkie, the founder of Somleng. "Somleng" means voice in a local language, Khmer. Somleng is a system that lets an organization automatically make phone calls or send text messages to everyone in a community who has a cell phone. Sending calls and messages individually would be very time-consuming to do manually. Using Somleng, you can record a voice message and have Somleng make all the calls for you. You can also set it to send text messages and reminders. Charities in Cambodia and elsewhere use this technology to send vital messages to communities about floods, and about aspects of health care, too.

In Cambodia, people receive warning messages on their phones, using a system called Somleng.

Tsunami Alert

Tsunamis are huge waves created by underwater earthquakes. On December 26, 2004, an earthquake in the Indian Ocean triggered a massive tsunami. Growing to more than 100 feet (30 m) tall, it hit the coasts of Indonesia, Sri Lanka, the Maldives, and Thailand, killing more than 230,000 people. There was very little warning given for this tsunami, and as a result, many people were determined to improve the early warning systems for these disasters.

In the past, tsunamis have been detected by buoys floating in the water, which measure the change in the sea level a tsunami causes as it travels across the ocean. The trouble with this is that the wave has to be actually present at the buoys, and so is already on its way toward the shore. Tsunamis travel fast and can reach shore within minutes, so every second of a warning counts if people are going to move away from the shore and to safety.

The tsunami of December 2004 led to improvements in early warning systems, to help prevent such a tragedy from happening again.

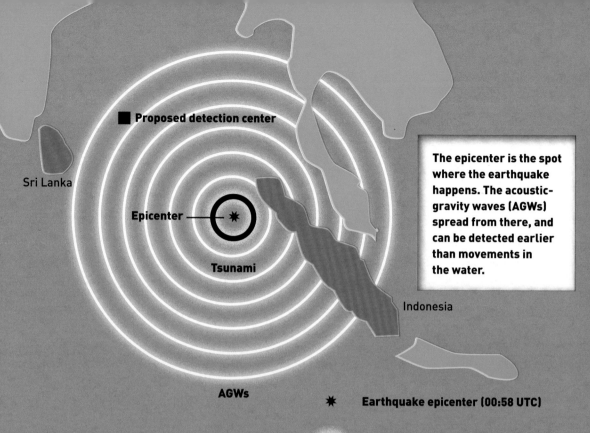

Proposed detection center

Sri Lanka

Epicenter —

Tsunami

Indonesia

AGWs

The epicenter is the spot where the earthquake happens. The acoustic-gravity waves (AGWs) spread from there, and can be detected earlier than movements in the water.

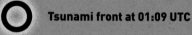 Earthquake epicenter (00:58 UTC)

Tsunami front at 01:09 UTC

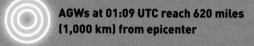 AGWs at 01:09 UTC reach 620 miles (1,000 km) from epicenter

The Sound of Danger

Chiang C. Mei, a professor of engineering at Massachusetts Institute of Technology (MIT), and Usama Kadri, a lecturer of applied mathematics at Cardiff University in Wales, have developed a new method for detecting tsunamis. Their technology uses underwater sound waves, known as acoustic-gravity waves (AGWs). AGWs spread out through the water from the site of an earthquake when it happens. They travel ten times faster through the water than the tsunami wave, so being able to pick them up gives the experts much more warning of what is coming. The AGWs may reach the shore tens of minutes ahead of the tsunami. This could then trigger an alarm, warning people.

The technology uses hydrophones, which are standard underwater microphones, to record the sound waves at an early stage. The waves are then tracked as they travel, giving vital information on the direction of the tsunami that is following them. Complex math is then used to analyze the data about the sound waves, and the earthquake that caused them, such as its location, length, width, duration, speed, and direction. This allows them to give a more accurate estimate not only of when the tsunami will strike, but also of its size and power, and all in 10 minutes.

CHAPTER 2

A COORDINATED RESPONSE

In the time immediately after a natural disaster, there is chaos. Power supplies may have been cut, buildings may have collapsed, and roads may have been made impassable. Thousands of local people will often have had to leave their homes and will be wandering the streets or the countryside. In order to bring some order to this chaos, it is essential for the responders to be able to coordinate their response and to work together.

Understanding the Disaster

The first priority for responders is to understand the scale of the problem to be dealt with. They need to know how large an area is affected, how severe the damage is, and how many people have been displaced or injured.

Recovers

Technology is being created and used to coordinate responses to disasters. One example was a direct result of the experience of two sisters, Morgan and Caitria O'Neill. In 2011, a severe tornado struck their family's home in Western Massachusetts. They saw the difficulty of matching offers of help with the people and places that needed it most, so they founded an organization called Recovers.

Rescuers urgently search for people trapped in fallen buildings. They hope to recover as many survivors as possible.

To help coordinators find the closest emergency response team to people in need, teams carry global positioning system (GPS) units. These use satellite technology to pinpoint their location.

Recovers is a web-based platform that coordinates the supply of relief effort with the people in need. After superstorm Sandy hit Manhattan in 2012, Recovers was working within a few hours. Relief workers posted their needs online, and suppliers and volunteers posted their offers of help. The two groups were very soon working together to help people in crisis. Recovers has worked in more than 40 communities around the world. Morgan and Caitria won a Toyota Mothers of Invention Award for their innovative idea. These awards are given to women who are driving positive change in the world, through innovation, entrepreneurship, and invention.

INGENIOUS INNOVATIONS

Another innovative way to understand the scale of a disaster is to use drones. Drones are unmanned aircraft that are controlled from the ground. Fitted with cameras, they can survey a disaster zone and provide essential information. Hurricane Irma was one of the most powerful storms ever seen in the Atlantic Ocean. It made landfall in Florida on August 30, 2017, causing catastrophic damage. The Air National Guard and Florida Power and Light both used drones to assess the damaged area, for the search and rescue of people, and to help restore the power supply.

Flowminder

Every year, natural disasters displace 20 to 30 million people. During large disasters and crises, there is a severe lack of basic information on the locations of affected people. This prevents relief organizations from delivering the correct amount of supplies to the right places. Researchers in Sweden have pioneered a new method to help track the locations of these displaced people and set up an organization called Flowminder.

In 2010, a massive earthquake hit Haiti in the Caribbean. It caused a vast amount of damage and forced hundreds of thousands of people to flee their homes. Linus Bengtsson and Xin Lu, two of the founders of Flowminder, wondered if it could be possible to use data from people's cell phones to help track them.

Thousands of people were made homeless in Haiti's capital Port-au-Prince when the earthquake hit in 2010.

Phone Tech

Anyone with a phone pays for it through an operator. These operators have many thousands of customers, and collect data every day about how their phones are being used. Flowminder uses this data from the operators to estimate the movements of people. The people monitored are protected because the data is anonymous, which means that individuals cannot be identified. But in an emergency situation, it shows the displacement of people in general.

In Haiti, this technique allowed the relief agencies and the government to understand where hundreds of thousands of people were moving. They could then be reached with relief aid.

Later that year, when there was a severe outbreak of a disease called cholera in Haiti, Flowminder supported the relief efforts by showing how people were spreading out from the affected area. They could be reached to prevent the disease spreading.

Nepal

On April 25, 2015, an earthquake hit the country of Nepal, in Asia. After the initial quake, there were more than 300 aftershocks that caused even more damage and panic. About 9,000 people lost their lives, and many thousands lost their homes and fled the affected areas. Flowminder supported the relief efforts again. Using cell phone operator data, Flowminder was able to show that about 500,000 people were on the move in and around the affected area, and where they were traveling to seek refuge. This was very valuable information for the relief agencies in the area, who then knew where to target their work.

Flowminder created this map to show the flow of people away from the site of the 2015 earthquake in Nepal.

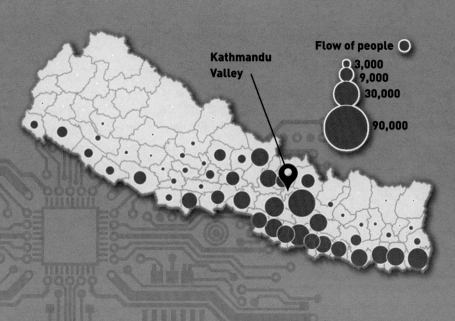

Kathmandu Valley

Flow of people
3,000
9,000
30,000
90,000

CHAPTER 3

SHELTER

The most urgent need for people whose homes have been destroyed by a natural disaster is to find shelter. After an earthquake, hurricane, or flood, people are often left out in the open, vulnerable to the weather and to more harm from the continuing collapse of buildings. They need a safe roof over their heads. Many innovators have come up with ideas for portable, safe, and durable shelters, for all kinds of terrain.

Flat-Pack Solution

Shelters for emergency situations need to be easy to transport, lightweight, and long-lasting. They may need to withstand challenging conditions, such as difficult terrain and extreme weather. The obvious solution is to use tents because tents are quick to assemble and cheap to produce. However, once the emergency has passed, the tents need to be replaced by something more durable.

The Better Shelter has a steel frame that makes it stable and durable.

The Better Shelter has a lockable front door to keep the people using it and their belongings safe.

One solution to this problem has come from the social enterprise Better Shelter and the United Nations Refugee Agency (UNHCR) with support from the IKEA Foundation. IKEA is a furniture company that sells most of its furniture in flat-packs (in separate pieces) for customers to assemble at home. This inspired the team to create the Better Shelter, which is a flat-packed shelter for displaced people. The Better Shelter is 188 square feet (17.5 sq m), fits inside two boxes, and can be assembled by four people in just four hours. With a steel frame, it is much more stable than a tent. The shelter resembles a house, with semihard walls. It has windows and a high ceiling, enabling residents to stand inside. An important extra is the solar panel on the roof, which provides power for lights and charging phones.

Using Better Shelters

These shelters are adaptable, too. Several can be joined together to create a medical clinic, for example. Each shelter should last for about three years, but even after the side panels have worn out, residents can still use the steel frame covered with materials that are available to them locally.

In the last few years, relief organizations have used many thousands of Better Shelters in their work to house people who have been displaced by natural disasters , as well as war and conflict.

17

A Fast Response

If you have been forced to leave your home in an emergency, as a result of a frightening natural disaster such as a flood, mudslide, earthquake, or volcanic eruption, you will desperately need a safe place to sleep. One of the most important aspects of providing shelter in an emergency situation is to provide it quickly.

Losing your home in a natural disaster is a traumatic experience and people need help quickly to find safety and shelter.

Safe and Sound

Argentinean innovator Nicolás Garcia Mayor came up with an ingenious solution. At the age of 21, he was a graduate student in industrial design at the Universidad Nacional de La Plata in Argentina. He wanted to improve the dignity and quality of life of people who have suffered through a natural disaster. He named his project Cmax, for his young brother Carlos Maximiliano. Cmax is an emergency shelter that combines the advantages of tents with those of trailers.

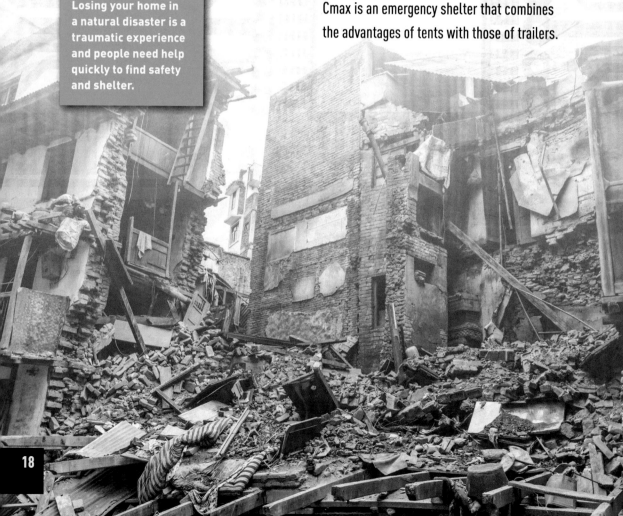

It ships and stores flat, like a tent, so it is easy to transport to the disaster area. Once there, it is quick to assemble: 2 people can set it up in just 11 minutes.

The Cmax has a solid floor, and stands raised above the ground on 10 adjustable aluminum legs. Inside, the shelter contains survival kits, collapsible furnishings, and electrical connections. Each one has enough space to sleep as many as 10 people. Garcia Mayor has presented his project at the Humanitarian Aid Forum in Washington, D.C., and at the United Nations (UN) in New York City.

INGENIOUS INNOVATIONS

Two British innovators, William Crawford and Peter Brewin, have developed a new material for making shelters for people in disaster zones. They call it Concrete Canvas. It is a textile that is similar to canvas but that contains a special mix of dried cement. When water is added to it, it hardens to form a thin, strong, waterproof, and fire-resistant layer of concrete. Essentially it is concrete on a roll. Using this material, Crawford and Brewin have developed an excellent shelter for displaced people. Everything arrives in a bag, then the structure is inflated with air and watered with a hose. It soon sets, becoming a spacious shelter that can last for up to 10 years.

It takes two people a short time to assemble the Concrete Canvas shelter. The fabric is then sprayed with water, which makes it set.

A Safe Place to Live

If the damage to the area around people's homes has been really severe, they may not be able to return for a long while, or even ever. In this situation, a longer-term solution for their housing is urgently needed. Rebuilding communities takes time, but innovators are looking for ways to make this happen as quickly and as safely as possible.

Shipping containers are in plentiful supply around the world, and they can be transformed into stable and secure homes in an emergency.

From Ship to Shore

A team of researchers at Clemson University, South Carolina, has come up with an innovative idea to provide safe, secure homes for displaced people. Their smart idea also finds a use for a plentiful product that otherwise would sit and not decompose, causing waste and pollution. These are shipping containers, the huge boxes that carry trade goods all around the world. They are made of steel, and measure 320 square feet (30 sq m). The containers are strong: They can resist winds of up to 140 miles per hour (225 km/h) and severe shaking of the ground.

With just a few modifications, this container can be lived in.

This makes them ideal for long-term housing, in areas where survivors of disasters may not be able to afford to rebuild their homes, such as poorer nations.

SEED

There are an estimated 30 million empty, unused shipping containers in ports all over the world. The team at Clemson University, led by Pernille Christensen, Associate Professor Doug Hecker, and Assistant Professor Martha Skinner, is working on ways to turn these into homes for victims of hurricanes in both the Caribbean Islands and the United States. They call their project SEED.

SEED shipping containers need some simple modifications before they can be used as homes. They need to be cut in a few places to allow airflow and to let in daylight. They are then coated with a special paint to add insulation, and fitted with wooden shipping pallets that act as "pods" for bathing and cooking. One more item is then added on the roof: 55-gallon (208 l) drums, previously used for oil. These can be filled with dirt and used as planters, for the residents to grow food.

In places that have suffered terrible devastation, enabling people to create homes that they know are secure and that they can be proud of, really helps strengthen communities, as well as ensures their survival.

Cardborigami

When you imagine a material that could make a great shelter space, you do not immediately think of cardboard. Surely this material that becomes soggy in the rain could not be suitable for providing housing for people displaced by natural disasters? One young U.S. architect decided that perhaps it could.

Tina Hovsepian was studying architecture at the University of Southern California when she came up with the idea of making a temporary shelter for the homeless that was lightweight yet strong, water resistant, and flame retardant. The result was Cardborigami. The name reveals the inspiration that is behind the design of the shelter—origami—which is the Japanese art of paper folding. The Cardborigami shelter works in the same way. It can be folded up into a small, compact size that can be transported with ease. Wherever it is needed, it can then be unfolded into a large, protective shelter.

Tina Hovsepian devised her innovative cardboard shelter while she was still a student.

From Folding Paper

Standard corrugated cardboard, the kind found in regular packaging, is used to make the product. It is treated with a water-resistant wax, and then scored with the lines that allow it to be folded and formed into a shelter. It is folded flat into a package that a single person can easily carry. Because Cardborigami is so light and flat, many shelters can be loaded onto trucks and transported to where they are needed urgently. Another advantage is that cardboard is a cheap and sustainable material. The shelters can be made from recycled paper and recycled after use. The impact of Cardborigami on the environment is therefore very small. This simple structure can make a big difference to the lives of people who suddenly find themselves without a protective roof over their heads. It is not a long-term solution, but an immediate response to an emergency situation.

Putting It to Use

Hovsepian's idea has had a big impact. Within months of it becoming public, she received interest from 92 different countries. When an earthquake hit Nepal in 2015, Cardborigami worked with the America Nepal Society of California and Wellabon to provide Cardborigami shelters and to help rebuild the villages that were badly affected.

Hovsepian has been celebrated for her innovation and has won a Toyota Mothers of Invention Award. She has also been featured by *Forbes* magazine on its list of top social entrepreneurs.

Cardborigami shelters are light and easy to transport, perfect for distributing quickly to a lot of people after a natural disaster strikes.

CHAPTER 4

SANITATION AND SUPPLIES

For people who have lost their homes as a result of a natural disaster, their second most urgent need, after shelter, is finding clean water and food. As well as needing water to drink, they must also have water for sanitation, or keeping clean and flushing away sewage. When this is not available, diseases such as cholera can quickly spread.

Sanitation Solutions

Unclean sanitation arrangements spread diseases, so many innovators are working on solutions to this problem. Peepoo is a smart invention that safely collects human waste and uses it as fertilizer. The waste is collected in biodegradable, portable bags. After use, the bag kills the harmful organisms in the waste that can cause disease. After eight weeks, the bag breaks down and the waste can be used as fertilizer on the land.

Peepoo is a simple but effective idea for making sure that human waste does not enter the water system and spread disease.

The ArborLoo is a composting toilet that costs just $5. A shallow pit is dug, filled with dry ash and leaves, and covered with a concrete seat. After each use, a cup of soil and wood ash is added to encourage the waste to break down. Once the pit is filled, it is covered with soil, and crops are planted over it. They are fertilized by the rich nutrients.

This tablet uses sunlight to purify water, to make it safe to drink. The process is quick, which is important in an emergency.

Water from Air

Watergen is an Israeli company that has invented cutting-edge technology to extract water from the air all around us. Watergen's mission, they say, is to use this technology to provide humanity with a new and renewable source of high-quality drinking water, made out of air, that can be available anywhere, immediately, and at a reasonable cost. This could potentially bring clean water to billions of people around the world. Watergen has developed an emergency response vehicle that is equipped with a generator, which they use in their process. The generator does not need to be connected to the electricity grid, and can be used in remote locations and in almost all weather conditions. The machine takes the moisture out of the air and converts it into clean water.

INGENIOUS INNOVATIONS

Sometimes there is no clean water supply, so the water that is available must be made safe to drink. One innovation for this can be used anywhere there is daylight. This is a solar-powered water purifier. Researchers at Stanford University worked with the U.S. Department of Energy (DOE) to develop this amazing device. It is a tiny tablet, about half the size of a postage stamp, that is dropped into dirty water and converts it into clean water. The whole process takes just a few minutes and the tablet is also cheap to produce.

Food

Delivering food to displaced people can be a real challenge. The normal infrastructure of roads and railroads is likely to have been destroyed. People may have scattered across a wide area, and be difficult to locate. Innovations in this area are making sure that these survivors can get access to the essential supplies they need.

Flying Food

The first problem can be transportation. One innovative solution is the Pouncer. This is a drone designed by British engineer Nigel Gifford. Its hull and wings enclose packed foods and medical supplies. It comes in three sizes, and can be launched safely from a distance, so there is no need to fly over a dangerous disaster zone to deliver the food. The Pouncer does not return from its mission. The main body is made from wood that can be broken up and used for cooking and heating. The wings, however, are the real innovation. Gifford is designing these to be made of edible material, so that they, too,

Natural disasters often destroy the roads and railroads that transport food and other essential goods. Innovators are developing new ways to keep the supply going.

can be eaten and provide nutrition. This is an accurate way of safely delivering food to remote locations.

Collapsible Trucks

Another innovative method of delivering food is by OX truck. This amazing truck was conceived by Torquil Norman and then designed by British automotive engineer Gordon Murray. The OX truck is made to be easily transportable, because it can be collapsed into a flat-pack. It is then easily reassembled where it is needed. Three skilled people can put one together in approximately 12 hours. The OX truck can tackle tough terrain, seat 13 people, and carry heavy loads of essential food supplies. The driver sits centrally, with a passenger on either side, to suit any country's driving-seat rules.

Nutritious and Delicious

The food that is delivered to a disaster area needs to be nutritious to keep people healthy. One Polish innovator, Alina Pelka, started a company called AidPol to deliver high-energy bars, freeze-dried fruit, and other emergency food. The contents of each food pack are adjusted to suit the dietary needs of the region, perhaps because of their religion or their health status. Each food pack also contains water-purification tablets and a kit for cooking. These lifesaving packs have been successfully used in many countries, including Kenya, Somalia, South Sudan, Guinea Bissau, Togo, Syria, Nepal, and Ukraine.

All-terrain trucks like the OX can often reach areas that are cut off from main roads.

27

Life's Essentials

Victims of natural disasters need many other essential supplies to keep them healthy and safe through the difficult times they face. Many innovators around the world are thinking carefully about the victims' situation, and ways in which they can help.

Comfortable and Warm

Sleeping out on the ground on traditional mats can be very cold and uncomfortable. One company, Charles Nielsen, decided to talk to aid agencies about what was really needed in emergency situations, and it came up with an innovative product called Life-Bed. Life-Bed is an inflatable mattress, with many air pockets to make it more comfortable. It is made of a material that absorbs the body heat of the sleeper, so it keeps them warm. It is waterproof, lightweight, and inexpensive. It is easy to inflate, and it can last for more than a year. Millions of these mattresses have now been used in disaster situations.

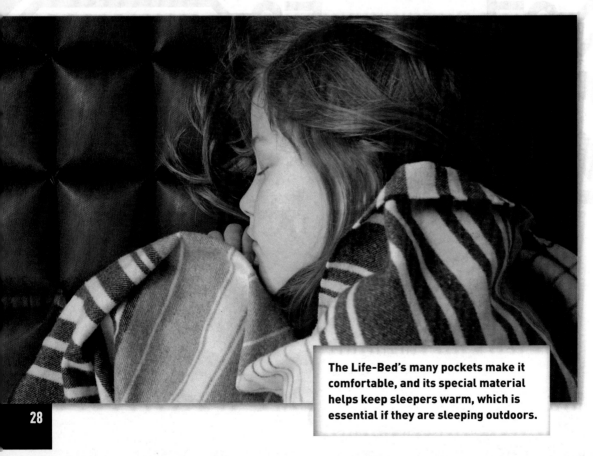

The Life-Bed's many pockets make it comfortable, and its special material helps keep sleepers warm, which is essential if they are sleeping outdoors.

Supplies from the Sky

In 2010, Jeffrey Potter witnessed the devastation the earthquake in Haiti caused. He was shocked that so many of the food and aid supplies that were sent from around the world to help people were sitting at Haiti's ports and airports, unable to reach those in need because of the damage to the country's roads. Tens of thousands of survivors lost their lives because the aid could not be delivered to them across "the last mile." Potter, who had a background in engineering, was determined to do something to help, so he created The SkyLife Company, which is based in Ohio.

The SkyLife Company's SkyPacks contain individual servings of medical supplies, water, and food. These are dropped from airplanes in Pop-Top boxes, which can each contain 80 to 100 packs. These boxes open out in midair, releasing all the SkyPacks, which float gently to the ground, providing food to a wide area. The packs can last for up to five years, so they are really valuable supplies. If larger or fragile items need to be delivered, SkyLife has developed a SkyBox. This is a bigger box that does not open in midair but has its own parachute to take it safely to the ground. It can land on a very specific drop location, to be in exactly the right place at the right time.

Flying food aid into a country is easy, but transporting it the last mile to the people who need it can be a real challenge.

DayOne Response

Having access to clean water is an urgent need for people after a natural disaster. Tricia Compas-Markman is a U.S. civil engineer, or someone who designs roads and bridges. Her innovative product can deliver clean water to where it is needed.

After college, Compas-Markman spent six years working on water-treatment technologies for developing countries, such as Thailand, Nicaragua, and Haiti. This led her to look at innovative ways to deliver safe drinking water to people in urgent need. She invented a water purification pack that she calls DayOne Response. This is a 2.5-gallon (10 l) personal water purification unit with a water filter inside it. The unit is built into a backpack, making it easy to carry. It is perfect for collecting water, transporting it, cleaning it, and then storing it until it is needed. The unit is also simple to use, which is important in the chaos of a disaster zone.

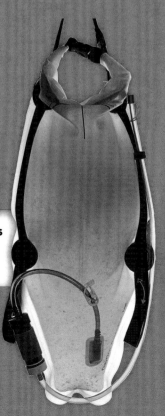
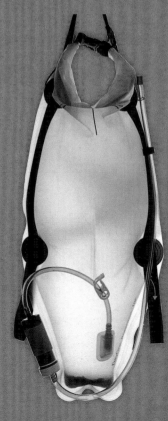

This before-and-after image shows just how effective the DayOne Response purification pack is.

Just one of these water bags can provide a family of four with clean drinking water for up to two months. It takes just 30 minutes to purify the water, removing harmful organisms that cause disease, and leaving clean water that is safe to drink and cook with. When it is not in use, the water bag folds flat for easy packing and transportation.

Success in Action

Compas-Markman's invention has been a huge success. It has been used in more than 21 countries around the world, in partnership with U.S. government and relief organizations. This portable water-purification backpack has been able to sustain families who have suffered terrible hardship, until their local water systems have been restored. For example, it was used in Nepal in 2015 after the earthquake, and in the Philippines after a typhoon. It has really helped Compas-Markman to see the bag in action, she says: "Being there is very fulfilling but it also gives us real opportunities for feedback. We can see if it is packaged correctly, learn about how relief organizations work and distribute products, and see how we can improve what we do."

At least 5,000 bags are in stock at the company's base in Oakland, California, ready to meet the needs of up to 20,000 people anywhere in the world. Compas-Markman has been honored for her entrepreneurship and innovation, and is the winner of many awards, including a Toyota Mother of Invention Award.

Many of those affected by the 2015 earthquake in Nepal were given DayOne Reponse packs to purify their water.

CHAPTER 5

MEDICAL TREATMENT

It is a sad fact that natural disasters injure large numbers of people at one time. Even reaching these people in remote areas can be a challenge, but delivering medical aid and health care to them is essential for saving lives and rebuilding communities. Innovators are using their medical skills, technical skills, and inventiveness to come up with new ideas to make this happen.

Medicines on Demand

One of the most important innovations in this area has been the use of drones. Rwanda is a country in Africa with few roads and no railroad system. It has benefitted greatly from the work of one U.S. drone company called Zipline, which is based in San Francisco. In October 2016, Zipline launched the world's first national drone delivery operation in Rwanda. Since then, it has flown more than 186,000 miles (300,000 km), delivering 7,000 units of blood in more than 4,000 flights across the country. It uses fixed-wing aircraft with a top speed of 80 miles per hour (128 km/h).

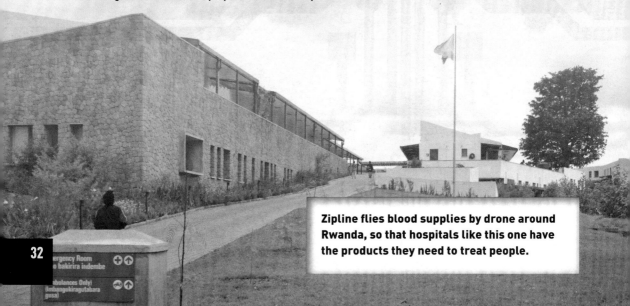

Zipline flies blood supplies by drone around Rwanda, so that hospitals like this one have the products they need to treat people.

Medical aid supplies are essential for treating people after a disaster, but many of them need to be kept cool to be effective.

Zipline's drone delivery has helped transform Rwanda's medical supply chain. Today, instant drone delivery helps ensure that hospitals always have access to blood products, increasing the use of some blood products by 175 percent, and reducing waste and spoilage by more than 95 percent. There are now plans to expand the service that Zipline can provide to the neighboring country of Tanzania. Indeed, the company's long-term mission is to build a network of instant delivery for the whole world. This ingenious solution delivers supplies to exactly where they are needed. Zipline is environmentally friendly, too, because, unlike regular planes, the electric drones do not use fuel.

Keep Cool

Keeping these essential medicines and other products cool in hot climates is another challenge that innovators have met. Ian Tansley is a British engineer who was determined to find a solution to this problem. He came up with the Sure Chill refrigerator, which uses ice and water to keep the contents at 39 degrees Fahrenheit (4 degrees C), whatever the external temperature. It can be connected to the power grid or solar-powered, and it can also keep on working for days without any power source at all. Sure Chill now has devices in more than 38 countries. They are helping keep medical supplies safe in all types of locations across Africa, Asia, and Europe.

Mobile Medical Care

Delivering medical treatment often requires a lot of equipment. To diagnose their problems, patients may require X-rays, scans, and blood tests. If they need to have surgery, the equipment must first be sterilized to prevent infection, and the patient must be anesthetized, or put to sleep. Their condition must be closely monitored throughout. How can you set up an operating room in an earthquake zone, or a place devastated by floods, where there is little or no electricity for light and power? Fortunately there are people working on the technology to answer this question.

Safe Surgery

Dr. James Bernstein is a surgeon with more than 35 years of experience leading innovative enterprises in the United States and overseas. He saw the need for a portable and affordable way to sterilize surgical instruments in remote areas without access to electricity, so he set up a company called EniWare to develop one. The company has created a sterilization box that is lightweight and portable. It uses a different process for sterilizing than conventional machines—a gas called nitrogen dioxide is released into the box and kills any harmful bacteria and other organisms on the instruments inside. The gas is provided in a pouch.

The beauty of this system is that it works at room temperature and needs no water or electricity to work. The only powered element

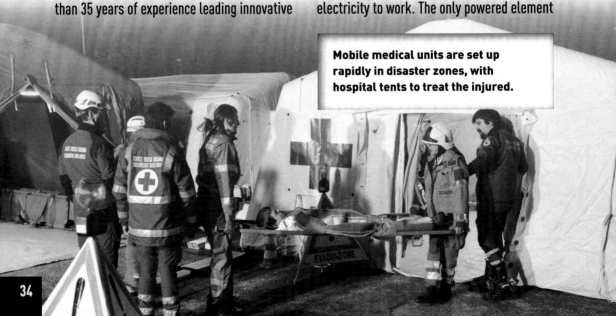

Mobile medical units are set up rapidly in disaster zones, with hospital tents to treat the injured.

is a battery-operated timer that notifies the user when the sterilization cycle is complete. Dr. Bernstein has raised millions of dollars to help develop this amazing product. It is almost ready to be sent out to the developing world, to transform medical care and lives, not only after natural disasters, but also in everyday medicine. When he recently demonstrated the sterilizer to a nurse in a remote hospital she told him, "Go away, leave now." This was not because she rejected his invention.

"No," she said, "we need this sterilizer so badly we cannot have you standing here any longer. Go away and don't come back until you bring us one."

INGENIOUS INNOVATIONS

Patients having surgery must usually be put to sleep. One company, set up by U.S. researcher and innovator Stephen Rudy, has developed the Universal Anesthesia Machine. Rudy started Gradian Health to develop safe surgery for developing countries. His amazing machine can generate its own medical oxygen from the surrounding air, for use in anesthesia, and it works without electricity. It is currently being used in more than 250 locations throughout Africa, Asia, Latin America, and the Caribbean.

The Universal Anesthesia Machine, which works without electricity, makes surgery possible for people in developing countries.

C2C

We have seen that shipping containers have been put to good use as housing for people whose homes have been destroyed by natural disasters—the size and strength of these steel crates makes them perfect for creating new dwellings in an emergency situation. One innovator, however, recognized that these shipping containers could also be just right for providing another function: delivering medical care to people in desperate need of it.

This pioneer is Elizabeth Sheehan. Sheehan spent several years as an aid worker, providing medical care in Africa and Asia. Having traveled to 50 countries to see firsthand how difficult it is to deliver medical treatment the last mile of the journey to the people who need it, she decided to act and founded an organization called Care2Communities, or C2C.

A simple container can be modified to make a clinic suitable for use after a natural disaster.

These Ugandan women are waiting to be seen in a pregnancy clinic, to ensure they get the best health care before and after the birth of their babies.

Seeing for Herself

C2C really took shape after Sheehan saw the devastation the earthquake in Haiti caused in 2010. Sheehan realized that communities there urgently needed secure, durable places where they could receive the health care that they so desperately needed. She thought that converted shipping containers could provide a solution. Sheehan gathered a team to help put her plan into action, and before long, her containerized clinic was meeting the needs of 40,000 people in Port-au-Price, Haiti.

The clinics are modified with windows and doors. They are cleaned and lined to make them hygienic for use as consulting rooms, treatment rooms, and operating rooms. After the initial response to Haiti's disaster, the need for more medical care remained.

Today, C2C runs four clinics, providing a lasting, reliable service to the poorest communities in Haiti. It delivers a full package of care, with expert clinicians, accurate diagnosis, and good supplies of medications.

Mothers and Children

One of C2C's main targets is to improve the health of mothers and children. Too many women experience health problems during pregnancy and childbirth, and too many babies and young children are malnourished, meaning they have a poor-quality diet or not enough to eat. C2C is carefully monitoring women before they give birth, and putting malnourished young children on a special program to feed them and improve their health. The success of both these programs is saving many lives.

CHAPTER 6

ENERGY

When a natural disaster strikes, it is not only buildings that are destroyed, but also the whole local power network often comes down. This can be very dangerous if it leaves live electric cables lying in the street. It also makes the relief efforts even more difficult. With no power to run heavy lifting apparatus in the rubble, and no lights to see after dark, many more people suffer, and many more lose their lives.

Battery Power

The solution to this problem of energy must come from sources that are off-grid, meaning not connected to the main electricity supply. After Puerto Rico was hit by hurricanes in 2017, most of the island's population lost power for an extended period of time because the power grid was badly damaged. Although the power supply has been improved, it still sometimes goes out completely. One well-known innovator decided to help. This was Elon Musk, the founder of the electric car company Tesla.

In San Juan, Puerto Rico, the hurricane brought down power lines and caused floods that lasted for several weeks.

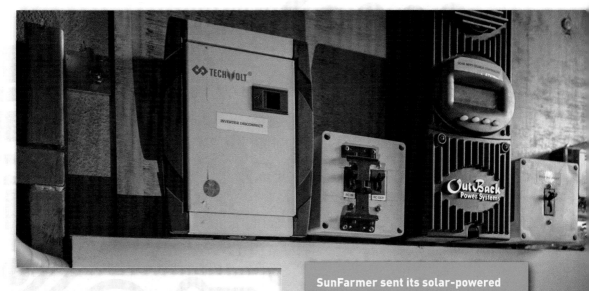

As part of the technology for their electric cars, Tesla has been developing batteries that can store large amounts of electricity. The cars need these powerful batteries to be able to drive for hundreds of miles without recharging. The electricity in them can come from the grid, but it can also be from solar power, generated by the sun. Musk helped Puerto Rico by sending them more than 1,000 batteries and solar-power devices. More than 660 locations across Puerto Rico were helped. They were chosen for the critical services, such as water pumping, waste treatment, and hospitals, they were providing in the aftermath of the hurricane.

A Long Story

Puerto Rico was not the first place where solar power was used for disaster relief. In 2015, when a massive earthquake struck Nepal's capital city, Kathmandu, a company called SunFarmer, which provides solar power and batteries to remote hospitals and schools in developing countries, sent its technology to fix street lights. SunFarmer also brought solar water purifiers and solar-powered systems to villages in the hills, which were hit hardest.

The first time solar power was used in disaster relief was back in 1988, when Hurricane Hugo hit Guadeloupe, St. Croix, Puerto Rico, and the southeast United States. The technology was way more basic then, but it was the start of an important revolution in generating energy in a crisis.

Harnessing the Sun

The last decade has seen a massive amount of innovation in solar power. Sunlight is turned into electricity using solar panels, in a process called photovoltaics, or PV. These panels are made using thin wafers of silicon, which absorb the energy in sunlight and turn it into an electric current. The technology behind these panels has developed fast, making them much more effective and flexible. This has given innovators plenty of chances to spread their creative wings.

The Fast-Fold Solar Mat from Renovagen can be carried in a truck to remote areas and then unfolded, to provide solar power instantly.

Power on a Roll

One exciting development comes from a British engineer and innovator named John Hingley. Hingley was interested in creating a device that can take solar power quickly and easily to remote regions. He also wanted it to be simple to set up and use, to provide power as quickly as possible in an emergency. He began work on creating a flexible solar panel, quite different from normal PV panels, which are rigid and heavy. Finally he came up with RollArray, a 0.35-inch-thick (9 mm) PV sheet that rolls up like a carpet.

This amazing invention means that a solar power creator can be rolled up, stored on a truck, and delivered by road or dropped in by helicopter to exactly where it is needed in the disaster zone. When it arrives, it is simply unrolled and, in a few minutes, is ready to start generating electricity.

No trained engineers are needed to set it up, so local people can look after it themselves. Hingley's company, Renovagen, has not stopped there. The company's latest product is a Fast-Fold Solar Mat. This small device fits in the back of a car, and in less than a minute can be unfolded and can start working.

INGENIOUS INNOVATIONS

One innovator wanted to solve the problem of displaced people becoming separated from family members and friends in the chaos after a disaster. Daniel Becerra is the cofounder of BuffaloGrid, which provides the power that allows people to charge up their cell phones in off-grid locations. The unit can charge 28 phones at the same time and contains a battery charged by solar power. Its built-in touchscreen can capture important information and send messages to areas where power and phone lines are unavailable. When displaced people have phones that work, they can contact family members and find each other.

BuffaloGrid helps people keep in touch by keeping their cell phones charged.

41

LuminAID

In 2010, when the massive earthquake struck Haiti, thousands of people were left homeless and were forced to relocate to emergency shelters. At night, these camps were blanketed in darkness. Two innovative graduate students studying architecture at Columbia University, in New York City, came up with a bright idea to solve the problem.

Andrea Sreshta and Anna Stork are the brains behind LuminAID, a company that supplies solar-powered lights to areas that are struck by natural disasters or do not have basic access to electricity. In 2011, the two women started testing prototypes in their kitchen, then traveled to remote villages in India to test the lights. They then launched a campaign on Indiegogo, an online fundraising platform, to fund their company. The support was overwhelming: They raised more than five times their original goal. From there, LuminAID was officially in business.

Sreshta and Stork hoped their invention would provide displaced people with enough light to feel safe and secure at night.

Designed for Disaster

There were several factors Sreshta and Stork took into account while designing the product. The lights needed to be compact, easy to ship, and simple to use. Each light folds into a small rectangle that is about the size of a smartphone. They are lightweight, weighing only 3 ounces (85 grams). A simple switch allows users to switch the light on and off and to control brightness. The lights are also waterproof and float when inflated, making the product ideal for emergency use during disasters.

While the LuminAID lights are being used in areas all over the world, Sreshta and Stork are still looking for ways to improve their product. For example, the lights are made from a material called thermoplastic polyurethane (TPU), which is durable and resistant to temperature extremes. The lights are also free from polyvinyl chloride (PVC),

which is a plastic that when produced and burned emits harmful cancer-causing substances.

Giving Back

When customers participate in the Give Light, Get Light program, for every light purchased, LuminAID donates another to a charity. The lights are distributed by nongovernmental organizations (NGOs) such as ShelterBox and Doctors Without Borders, in countries all over the world. When the light is delivered to the buyer, a sticker indicates where their donation has been sent.

LuminAID has won several awards for its innovative products, for both its renewable energy use and its global initiatives to bring light to those without it. Sreshta and Stork have also been recognized for their ingenuity: Both women were named Mothers of Invention in 2014 by Toyota.

INNOVATORS OF THE FUTURE

It is clear that researchers, entrepreneurs, large organizations, and governments are all working hard to solve the problems of people whose lives have been turned upside down by a natural disaster. This is a global problem that is not going to go away. Extreme weather events may become more frequent as our climate changes.

Rescue Robots

Some cutting-edge ideas are emerging in this complex field. One example is the WALK-MAN, a human-controlled robot to help with rescue efforts. Designed by the Italian Institute of Technology, this humanoid bot can go places where people cannot, such as unstable

Robots like this one will be used more and more in search and rescue operations.

buildings and factories after a chemical leak. It can navigate difficult terrain, find sources of leaks, and close them off. It could provide very useful extra help in an emergency.

A Network of Connections

One very important aspect of disaster relief is having good information. With the spread of cell phones to all parts of the world, and the use of social media, it is possible for the authorities to learn more about these critical situations, and faster than ever before. Real-time data allows the relief effort to be more targeted. Someone stranded in a house as it floods can send a text or other message to get help.

Being Prepared

We know that disasters will come, but not when. Being prepared is another important aspect of dealing successfully with a natural disaster. In fact, some say that what we do before a disaster happens is what has the greatest impact on changing its outcome. One U.S. company is innovating technology to make places as prepared as they can be. One Concern puts together a detailed picture of a location and its risks. It models the location's buildings, transportation systems, and electricity and water supplies, then looks for points of weakness. It adds data about its natural environment, such as climate and

One Concern produces maps from data to show areas of risk and how badly a place is likely to be affected by a natural disaster.

vegetation. Finally, it adds data about how people are behaving, using information from phones and social media. All this data builds a picture that allows experts to predict how a place will react if a natural disaster strikes.

Being prepared for natural disasters gives us time to become more resilient. We cannot avoid these forces of nature, but we can certainly apply our skills to minimize the impact they have on our world.

Glossary

anonymous not identified by name

bacteria tiny living things that cause disease

biodegradable able to be broken down naturally

buoys floating objects tied to the seafloor

cholera a disease that is carried by dirty water

composting turning something into fertilizer

corrugated strengthened by parallel ridges

data information

decompose rot

developing countries poorer countries that are trying to build their economies

displaced forced to leave their home

drone a pilotless aircraft

durable long-lasting

entrepreneurship having ideas and starting businesses to develop them

fertilizer a substance that feeds the soil and the plants that grow in it

generator a machine that changes movement into electricity

global positioning system (GPS) a system of satellites that can pinpoint the location of a ground-based receiver using the time taken for sound waves to travel from satellite to receiver

grid the network that distributes electricity from power stations to consumers

humanoid shaped like a human

hygienic clean and preventing disease

infrastructure roads and power supplies

insulation materials that prevent heat loss

lava hot molten rock from a volcano

machine learning programs that let computers remember and learn from past events

malnourished suffering poor health because of not eating enough food or the right kinds of food

microbes very small organisms such as bacteria

molten melted

nongovernmental organizations (NGOs) independent organizations that do not make a profit and do charitable work

photovoltaics (PV) making electricity from sunlight

platform a computer system

portable easily carried

prototypes early designs of a new invention

purification the process of cleaning dirty water

refugees people who are forced to leave their country because of danger

relief help and supplies

renewable a resource that does not run out, such as wind, or can be replanted

resilient able to withstand difficulties

sanitation arrangements for clean drinking water and the disposal of waste

social enterprise a business that puts its profits into helping people or the planet

solar using the sun's light to make electricity

sterilized thoroughly cleaned

sustainable a resource that is renewable or will not run out, such as plants or wind

terrain land and its features, such as hills

tsunamis waves made by an undersea earthquake

For More Information

Books

Maurer, Tracy Nelson. *The World's Worst Volcanic Eruptions.* North Mankato, MN: Capstone Press, 2019.

Rissman, Rebecca. *Swept Away: The Story of the 2011 Japanese Tsunami.* North Mankato, MN: Capstone Press, 2017.

Rusch, Elizabeth. *Eruption!: Volcanoes and the Science of Saving Lives.* Boston, MA: Houghton Mifflin Harcourt, 2013.

Spilsbury, Louise, and Richard Spilsbury. *Earthquake Shatters Country.* New York, NY: Gareth Stevens Publishing, 2018.

Websites

Discover more about Day One Response water purification at:
dayoneresponse.com

Read about Cardborigami and how it is used for shelters in disaster zones at:
www.cardborigami.org

Find out more about disaster relief at:
www.kidsgoglobal.net/the-issues/disaster-relief

Learn how to be prepared for natural disasters at:
www.ready.gov/kids

Publisher's note to educators and parents:
Our editors have carefully reviewed these websites to ensure that they are suitable for students. Many websites change frequently, however, and we cannot guarantee that a site's future contents will continue to meet our high standards of quality and educational value. Be advised that students should be closely supervised whenever they access the Internet.

Index